I0468754

Swearing Cat Patterns

SwearWord Adult Coloring Book

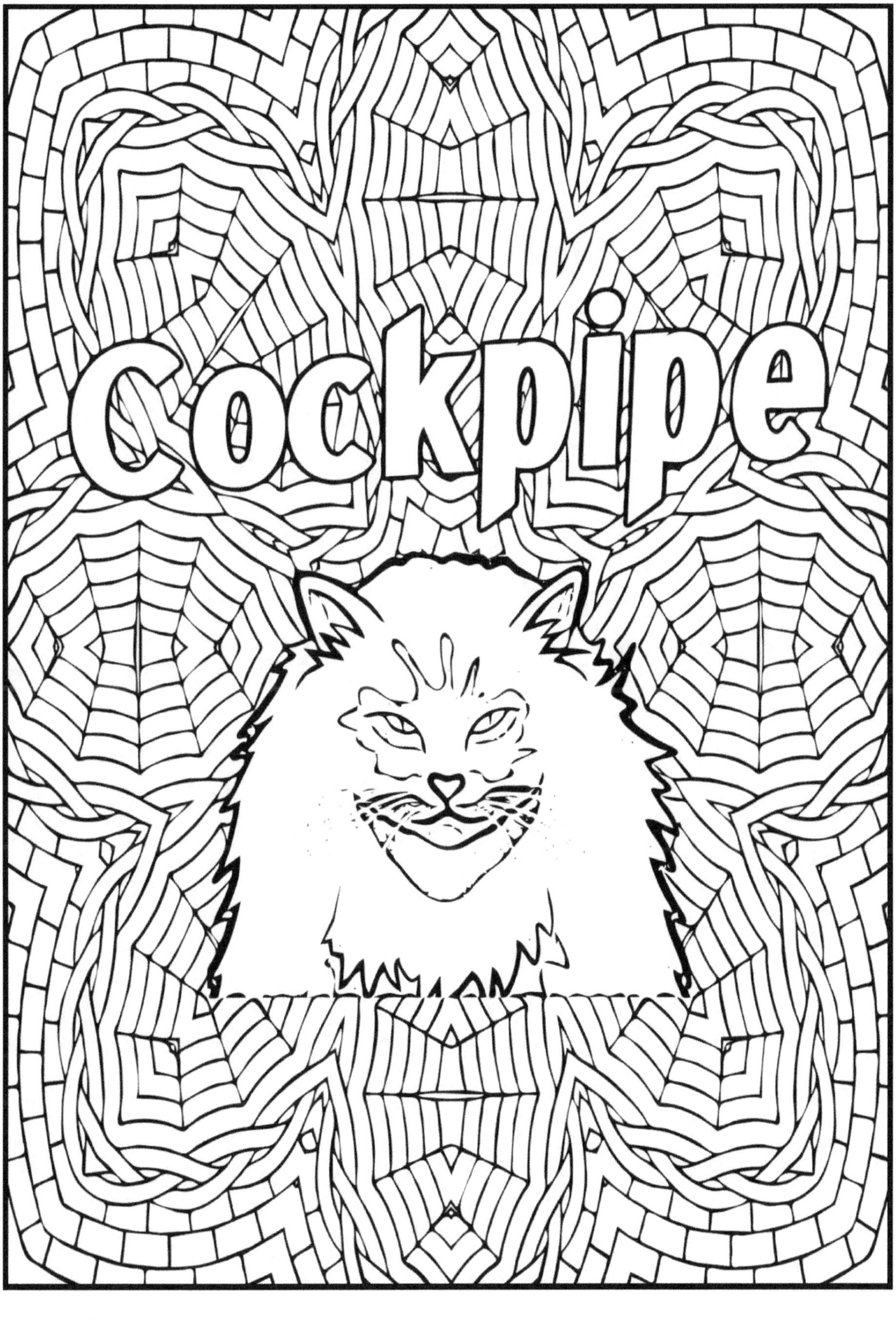
Cockpipe

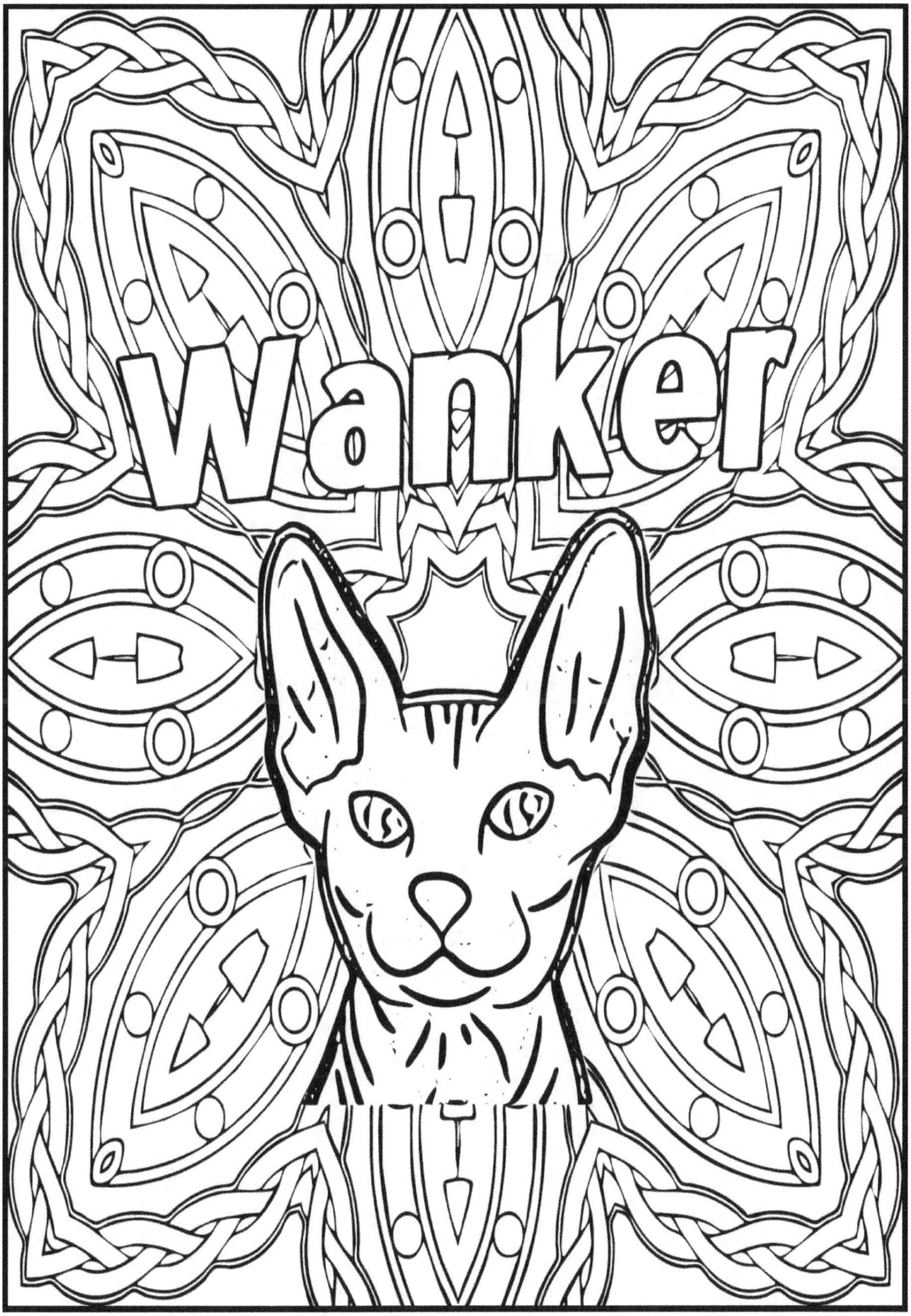
Wanker

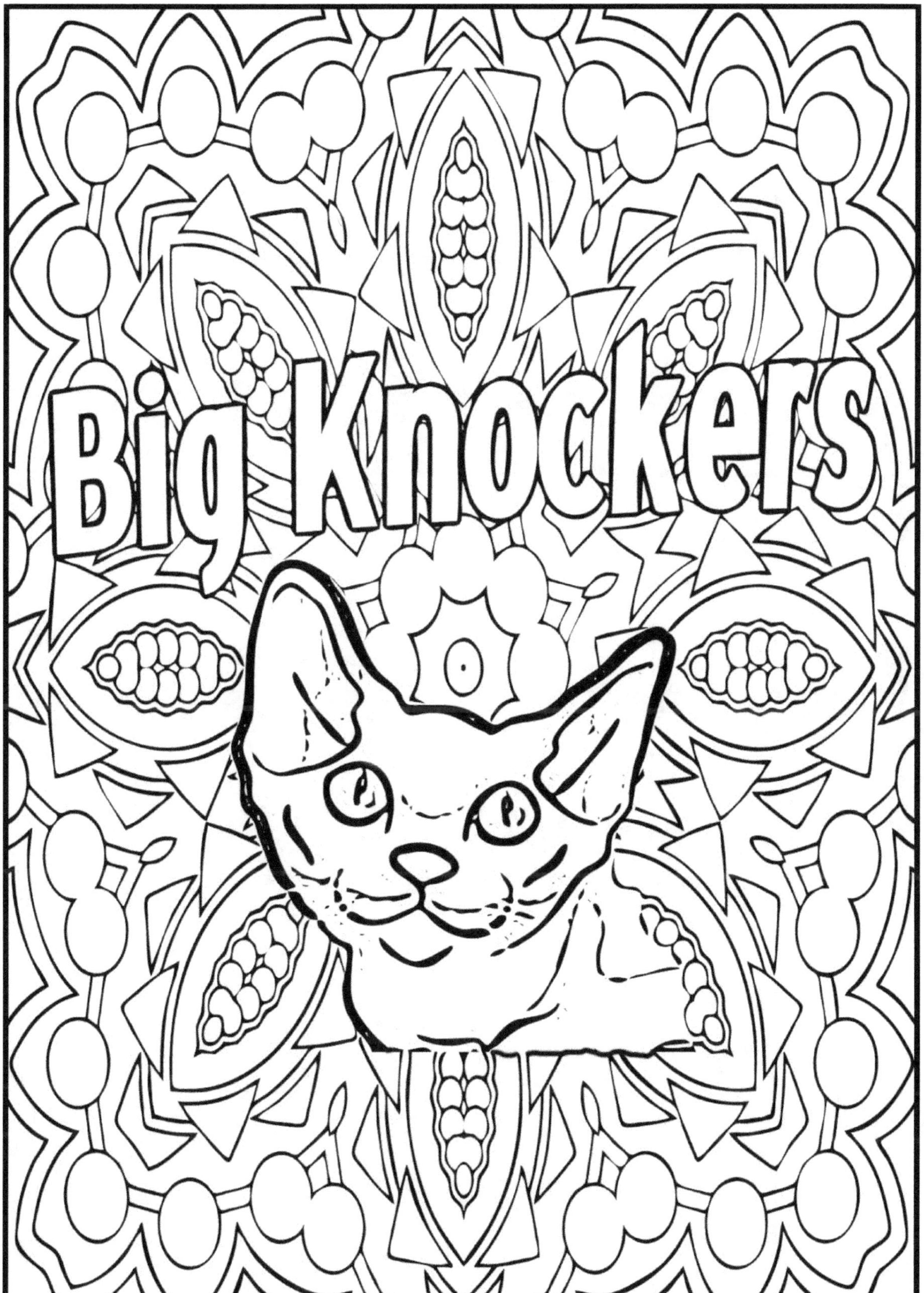
Big Knockers

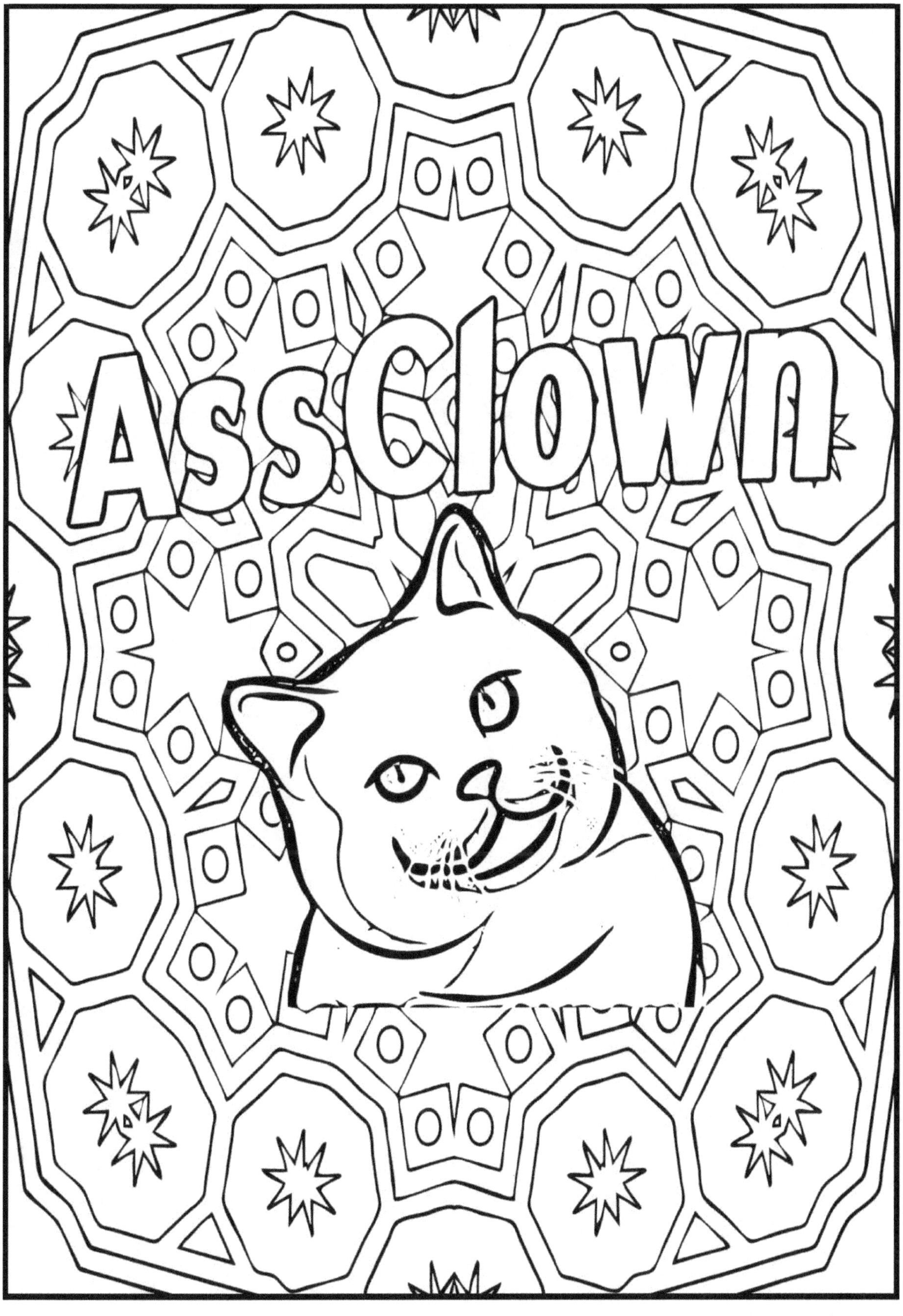
AssClown

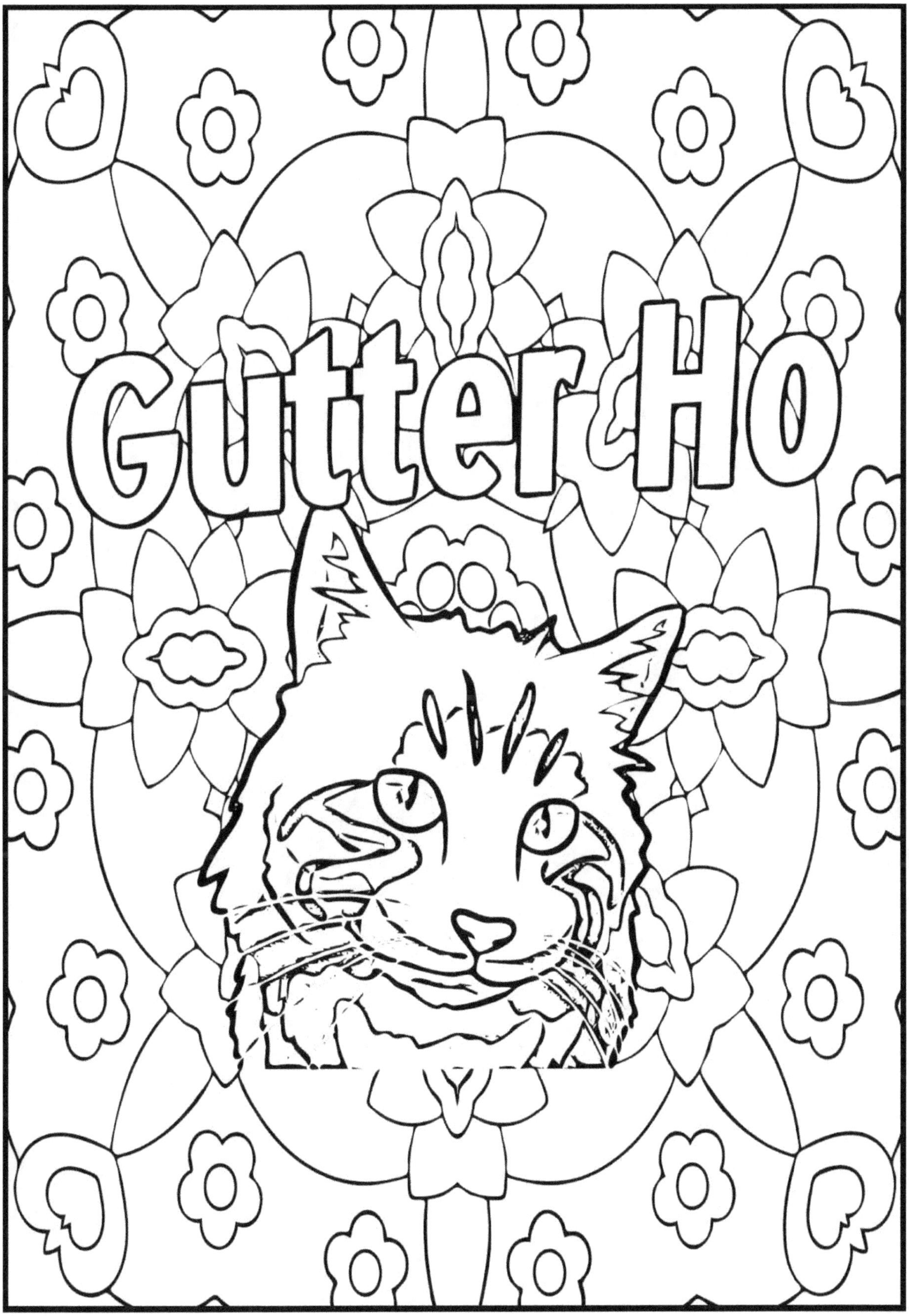
Gutter Ho

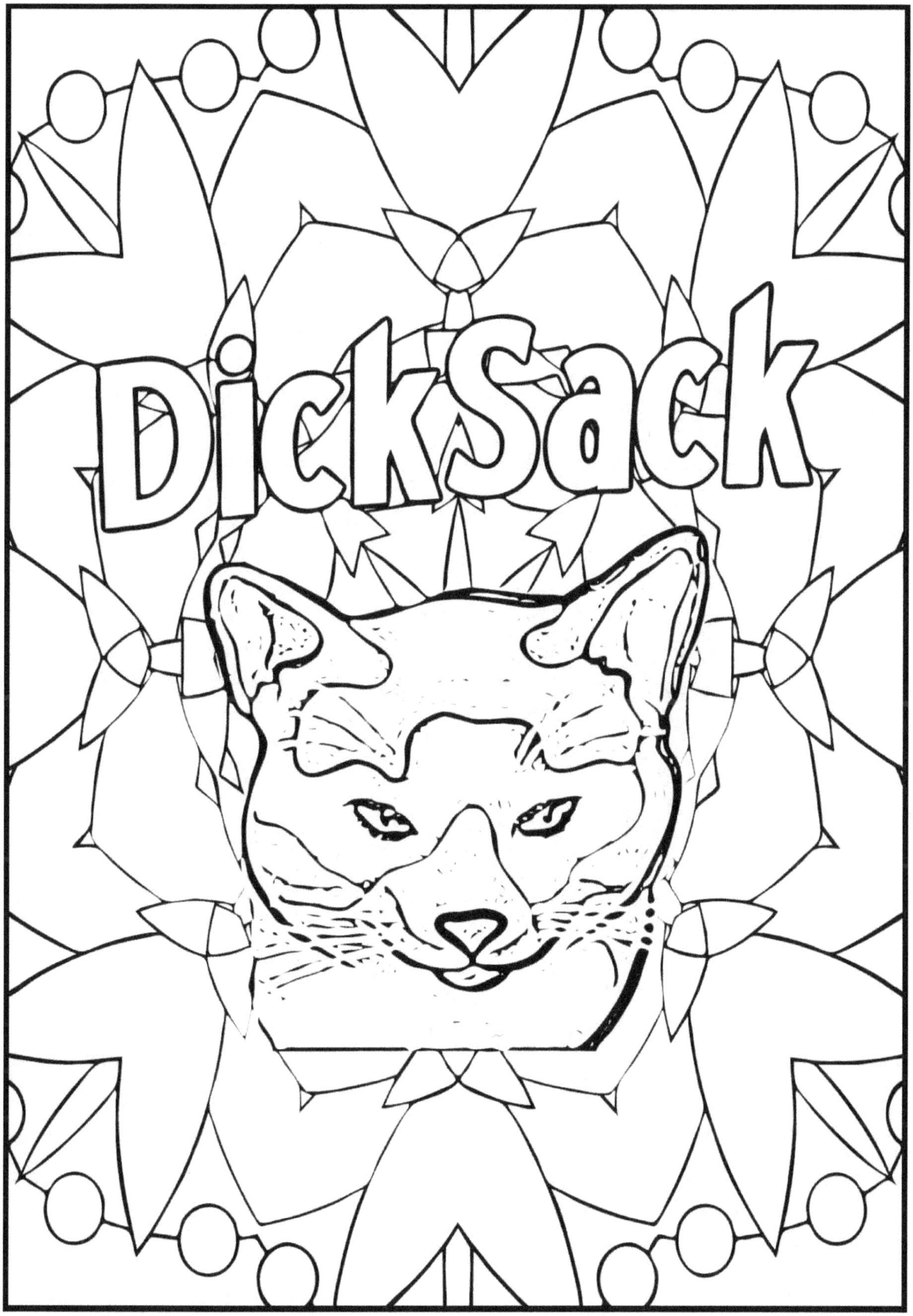
DickSack

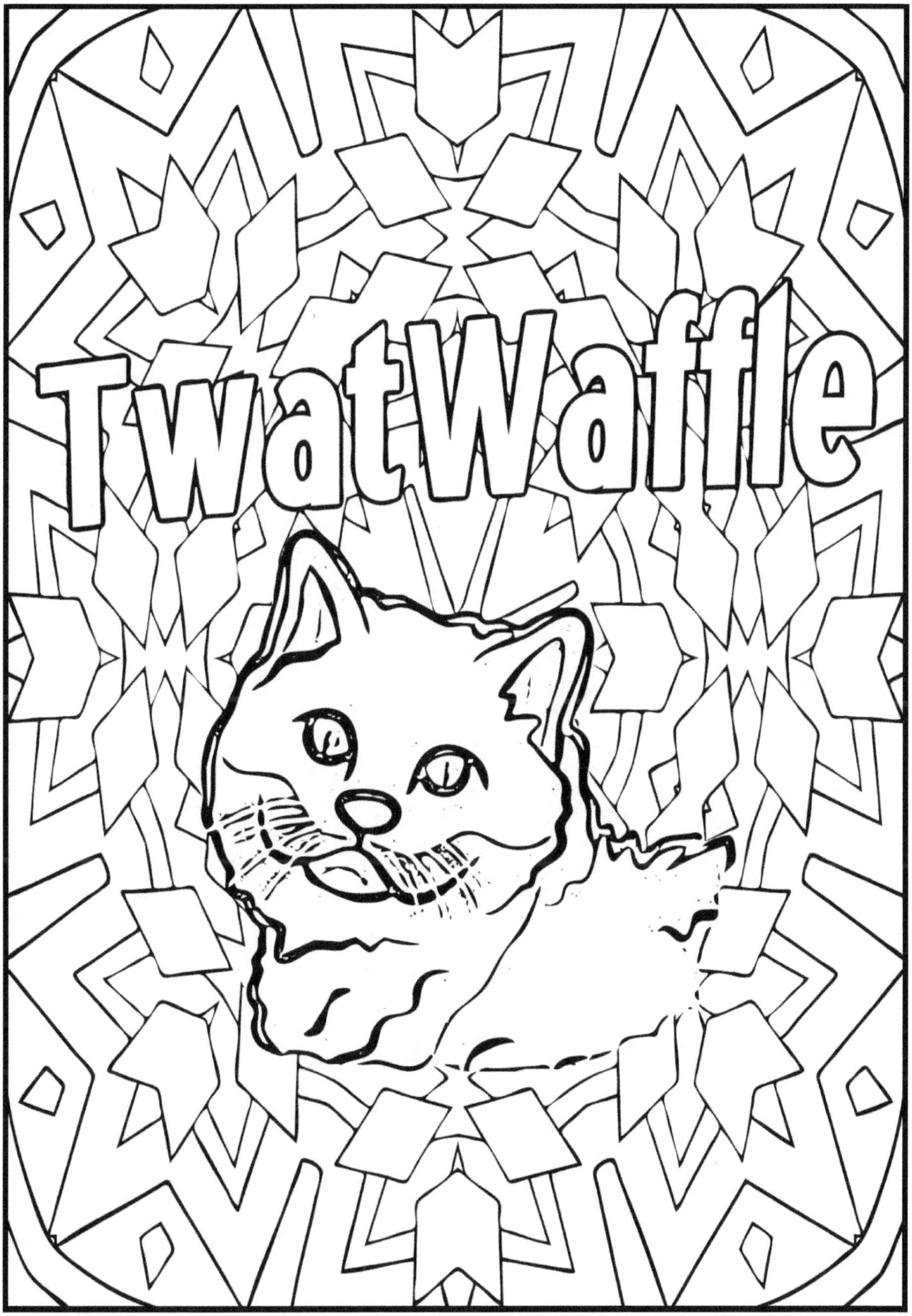
TwatWaffle

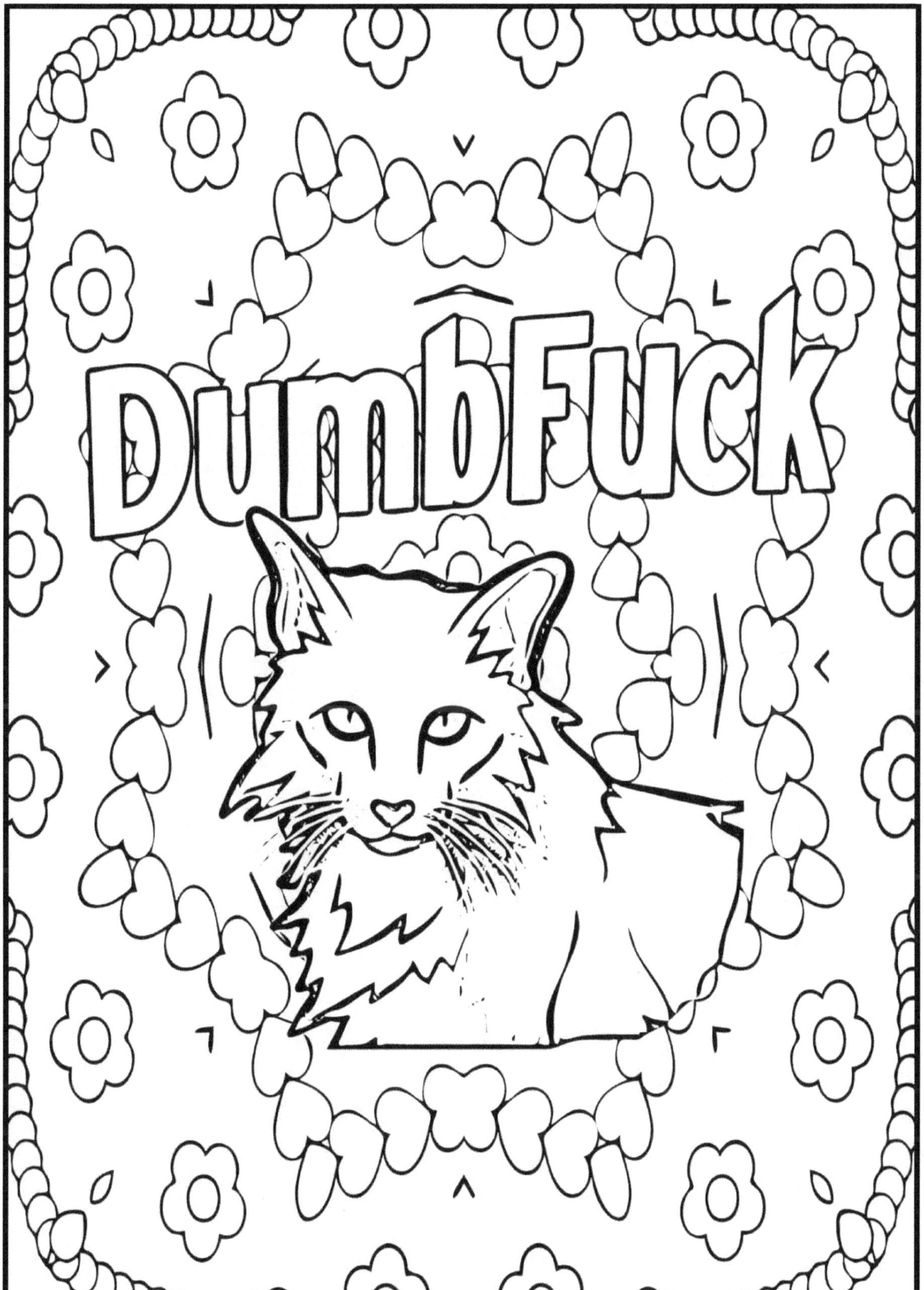
DumbFuck

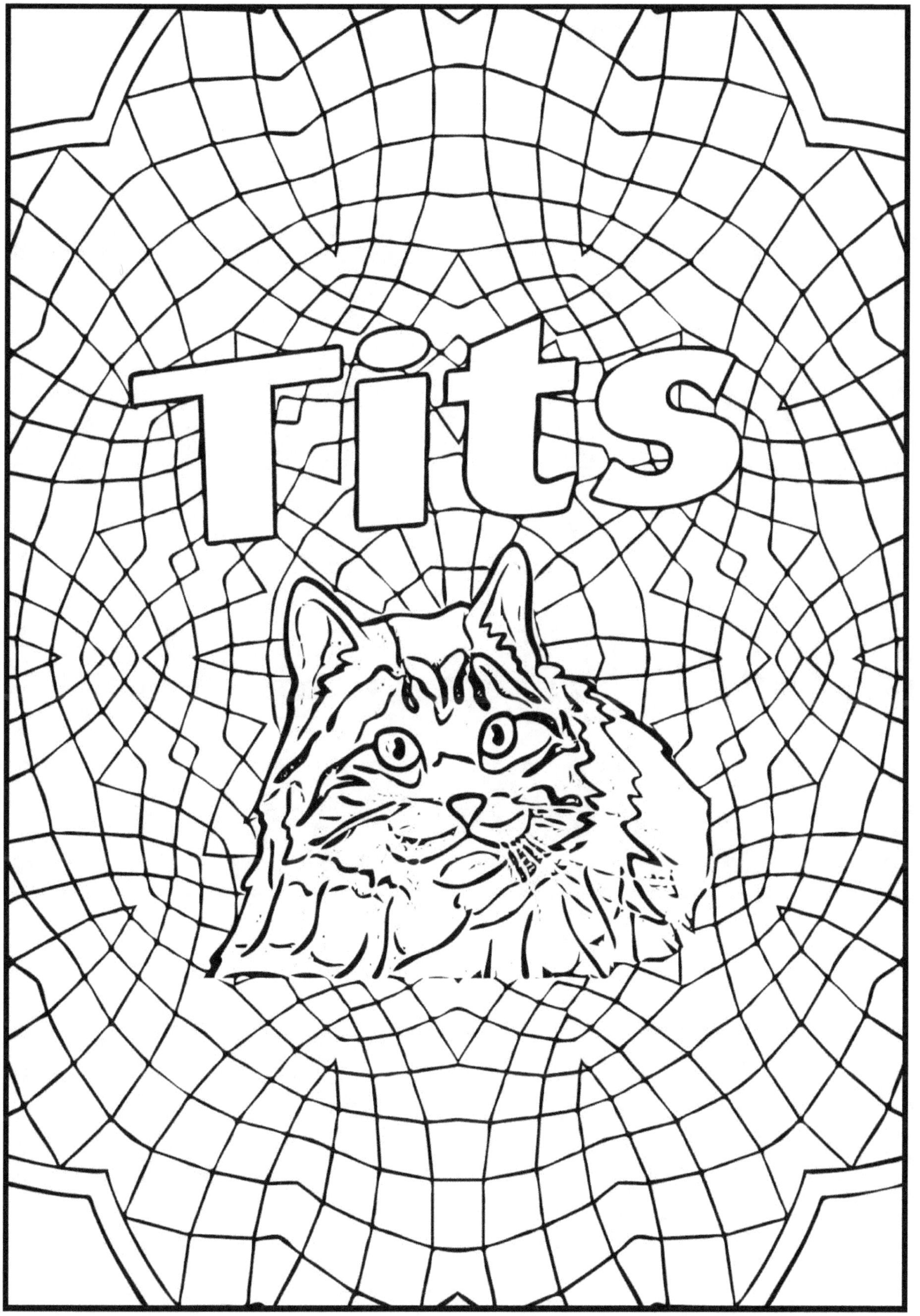
Tits

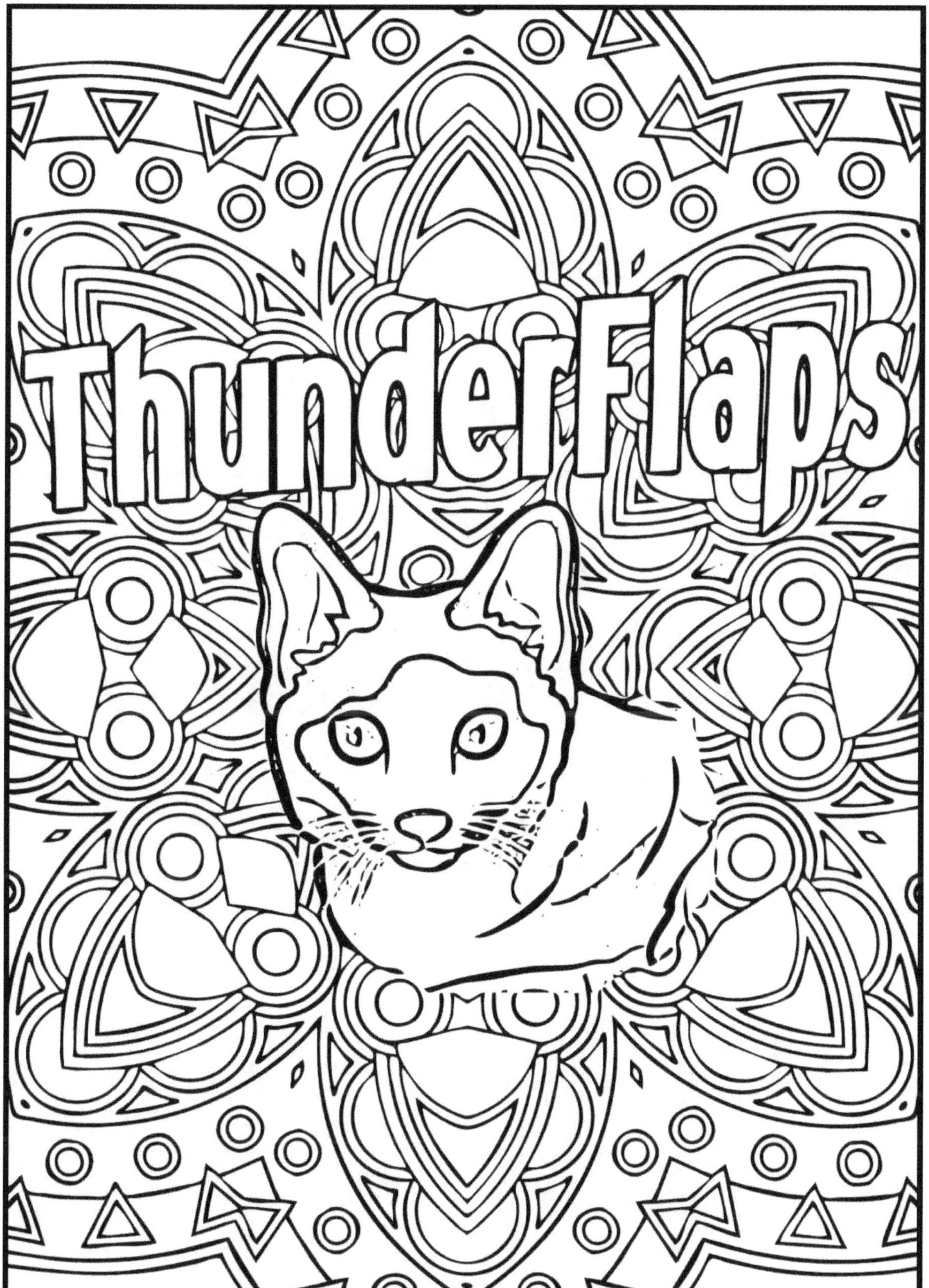
ThunderFlaps

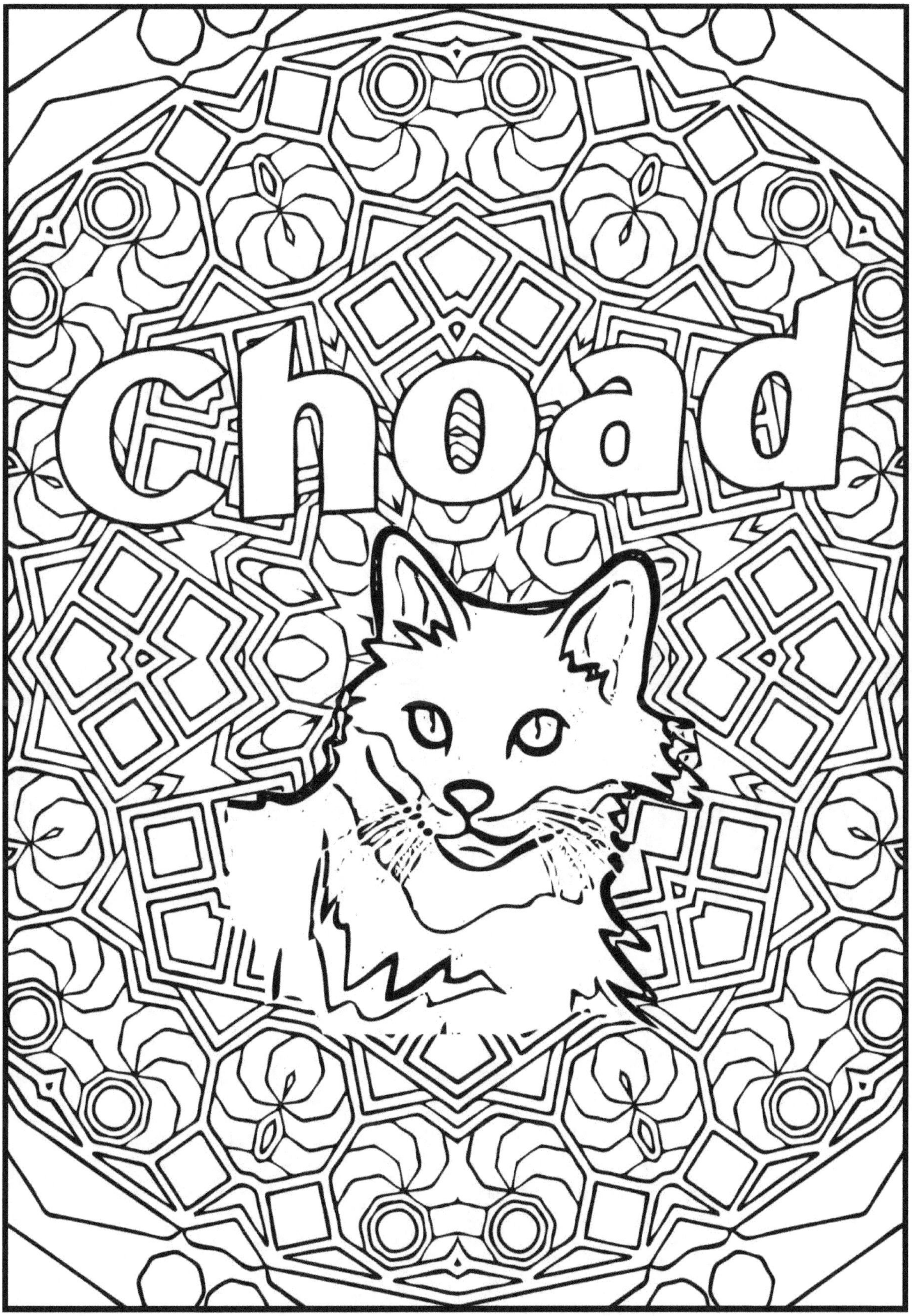
Choad

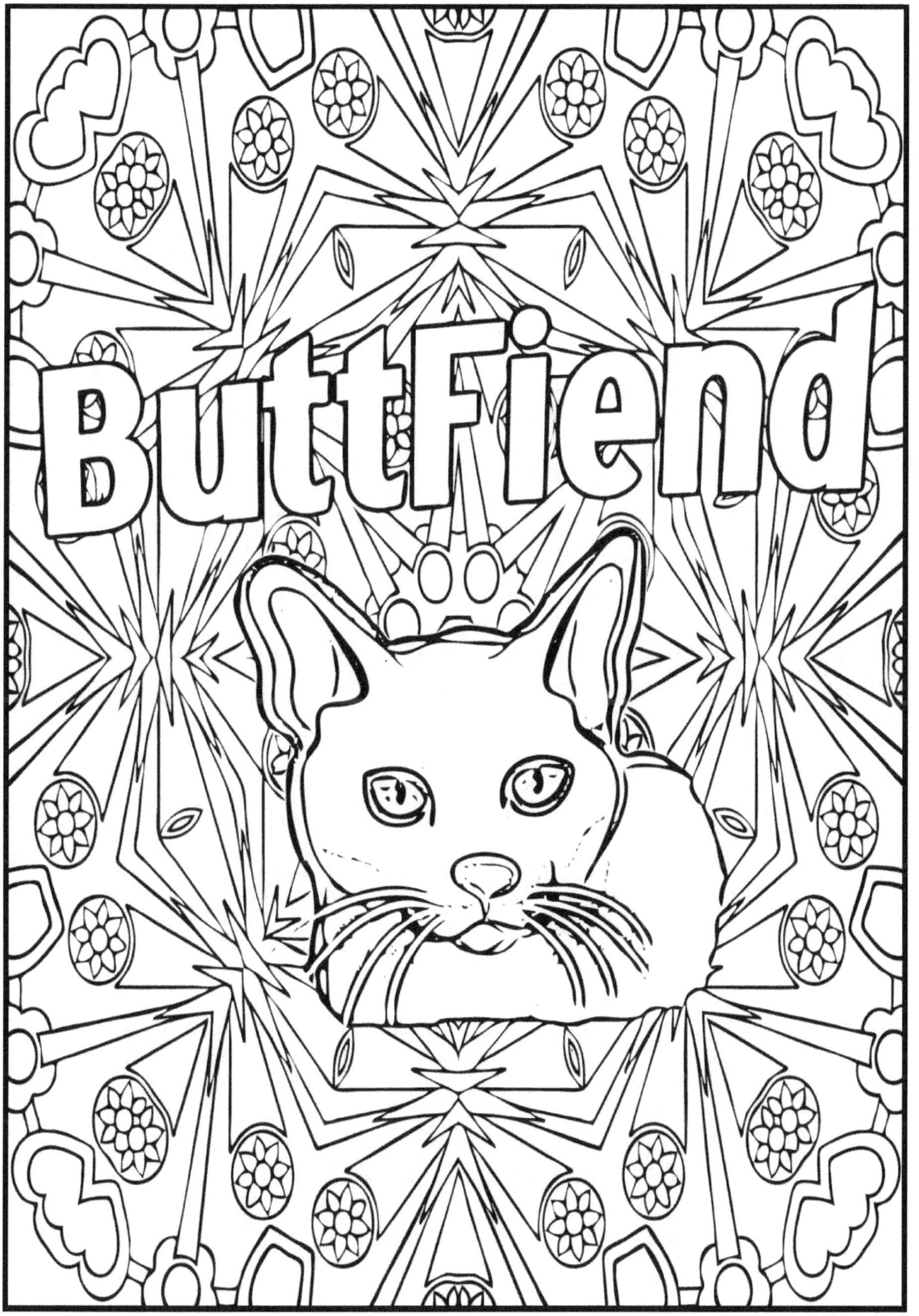
ButtFiend

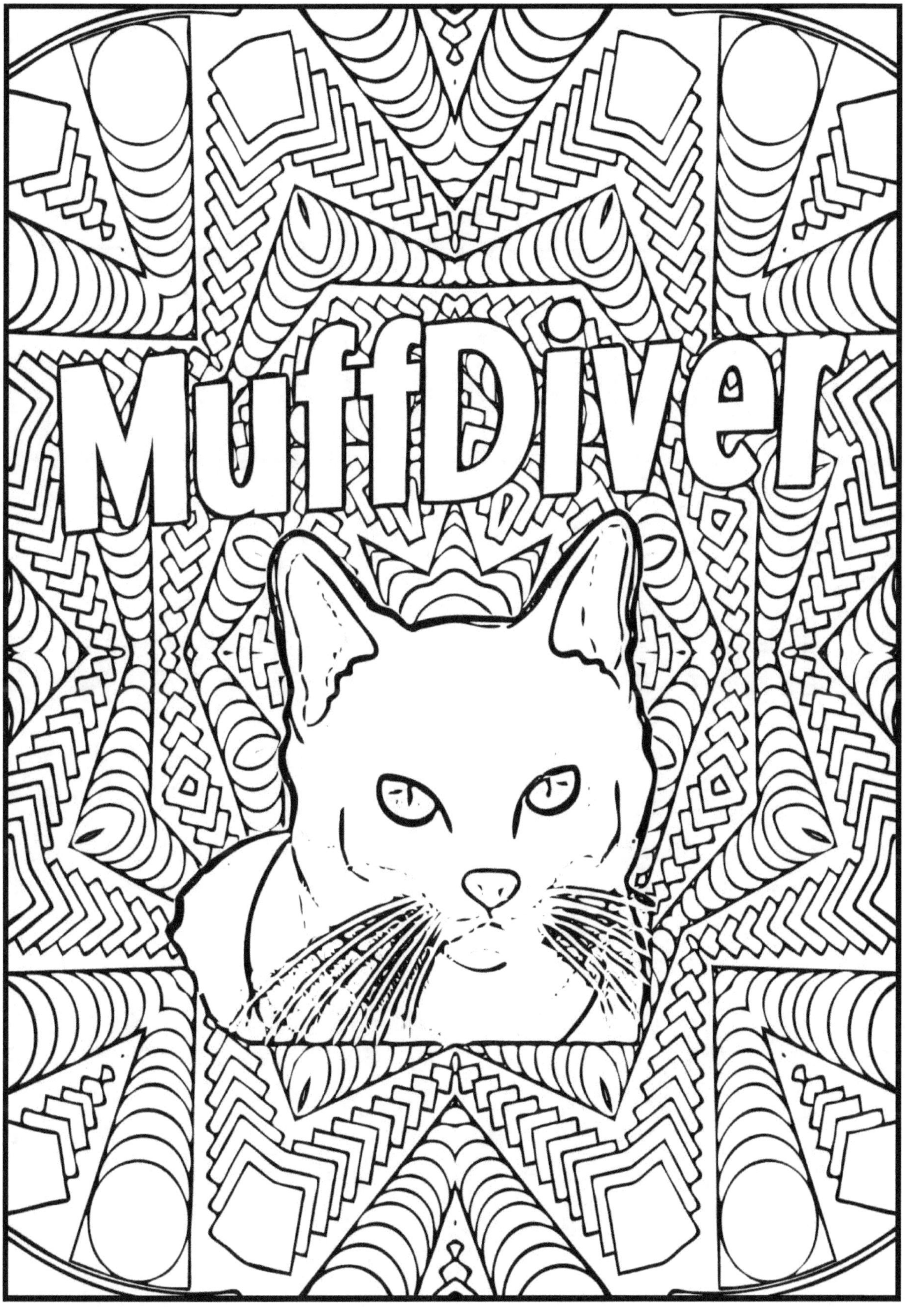
MuffDiver

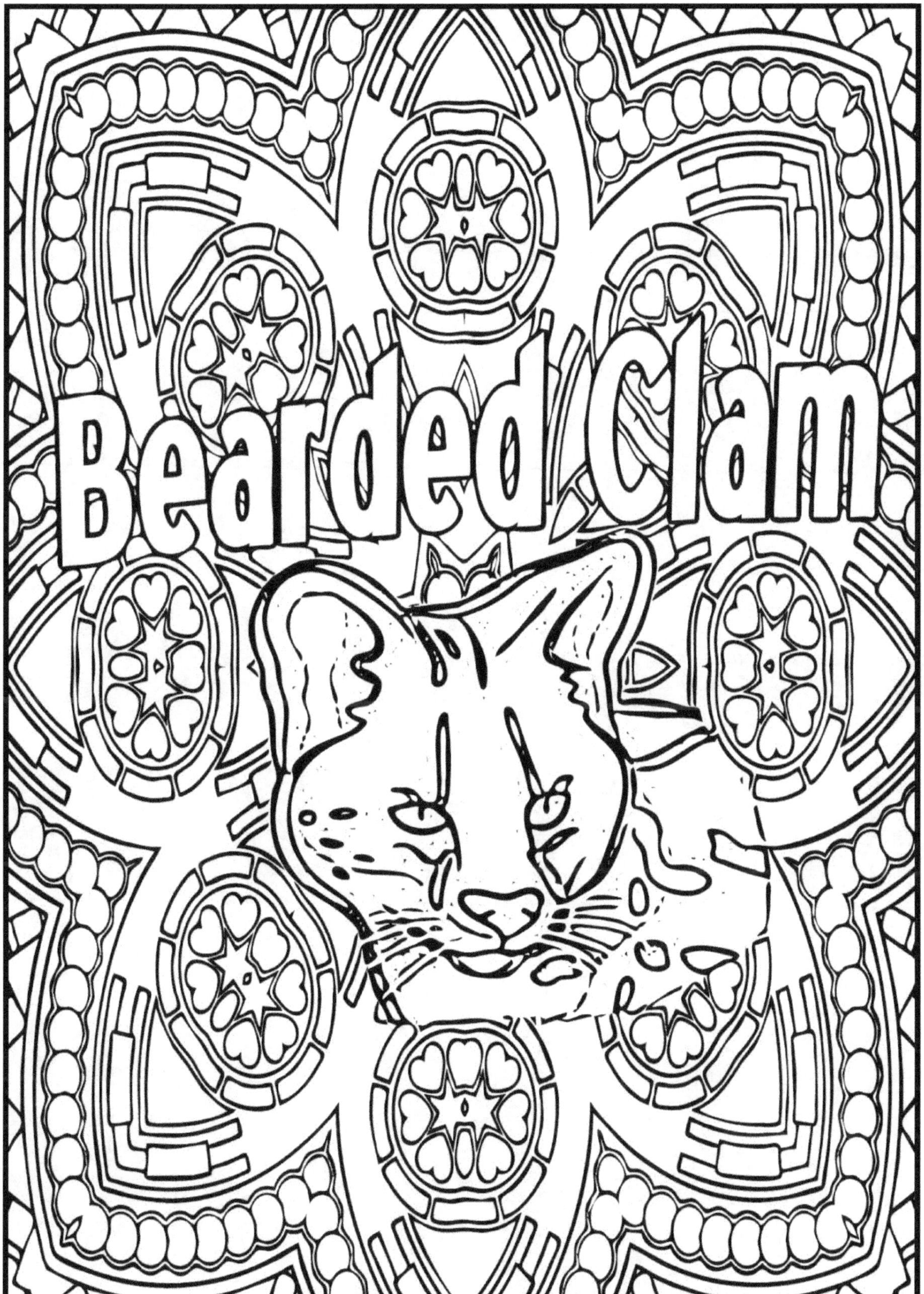
Bearded Clam

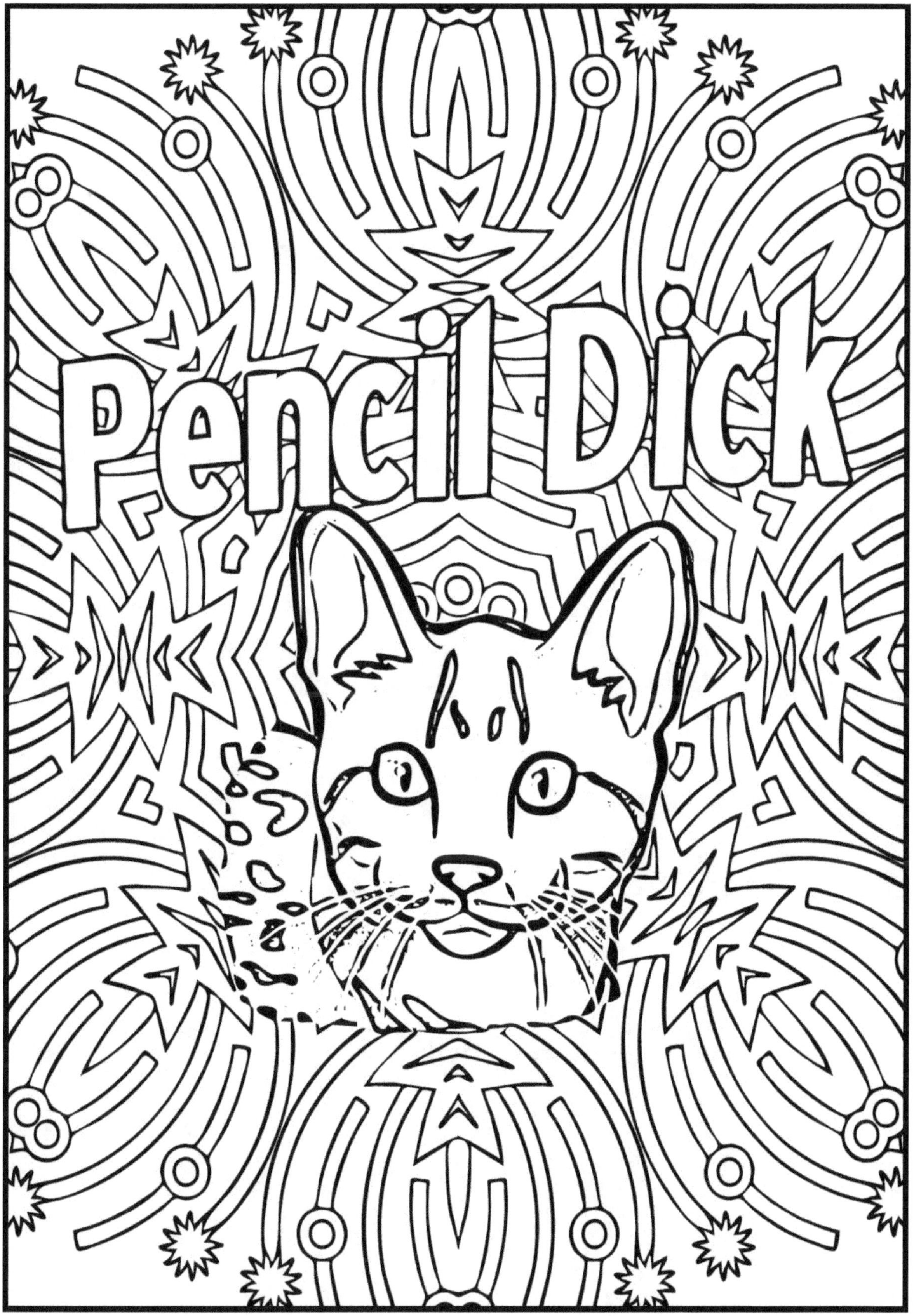
Pencil Dick

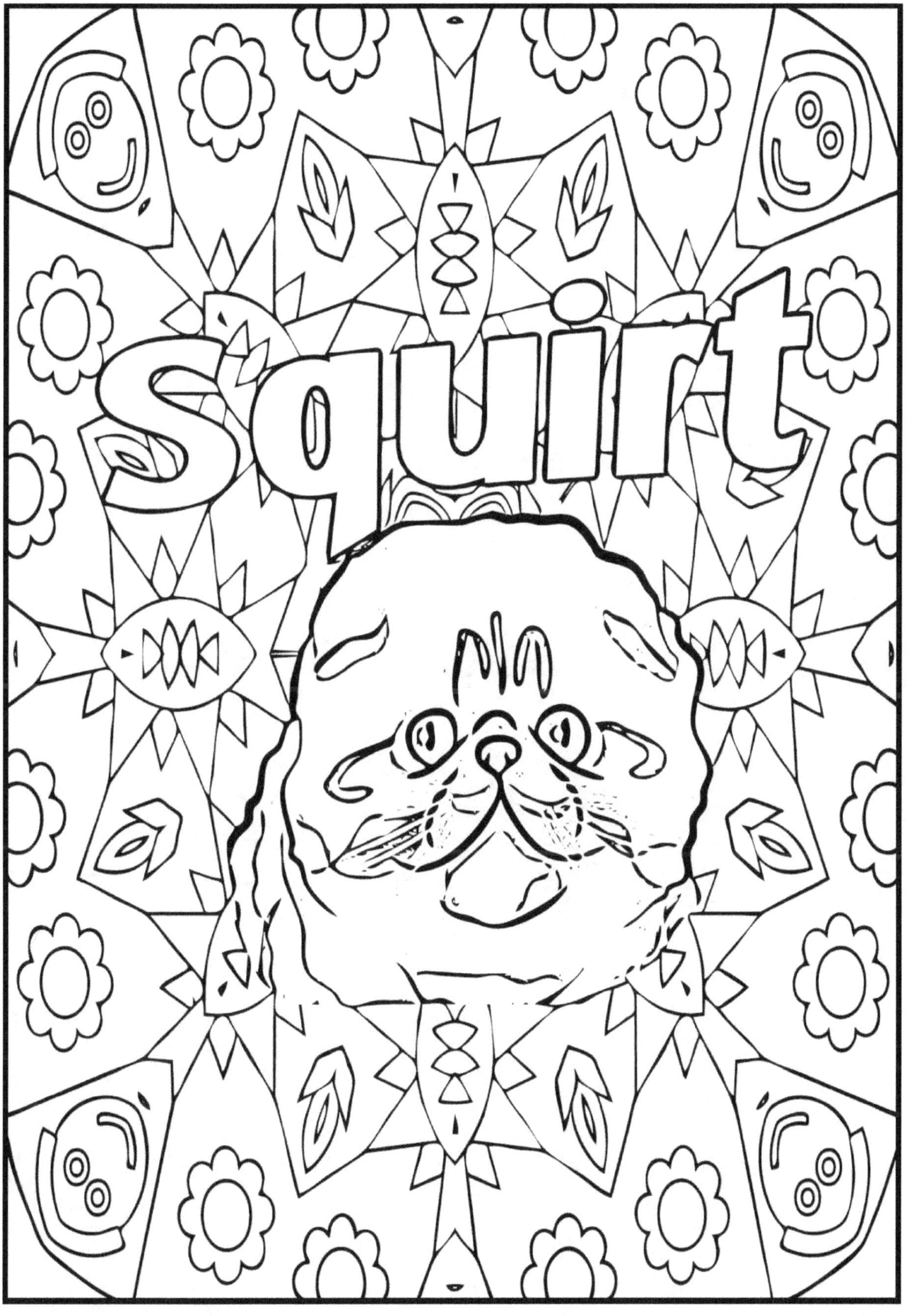
Squirt

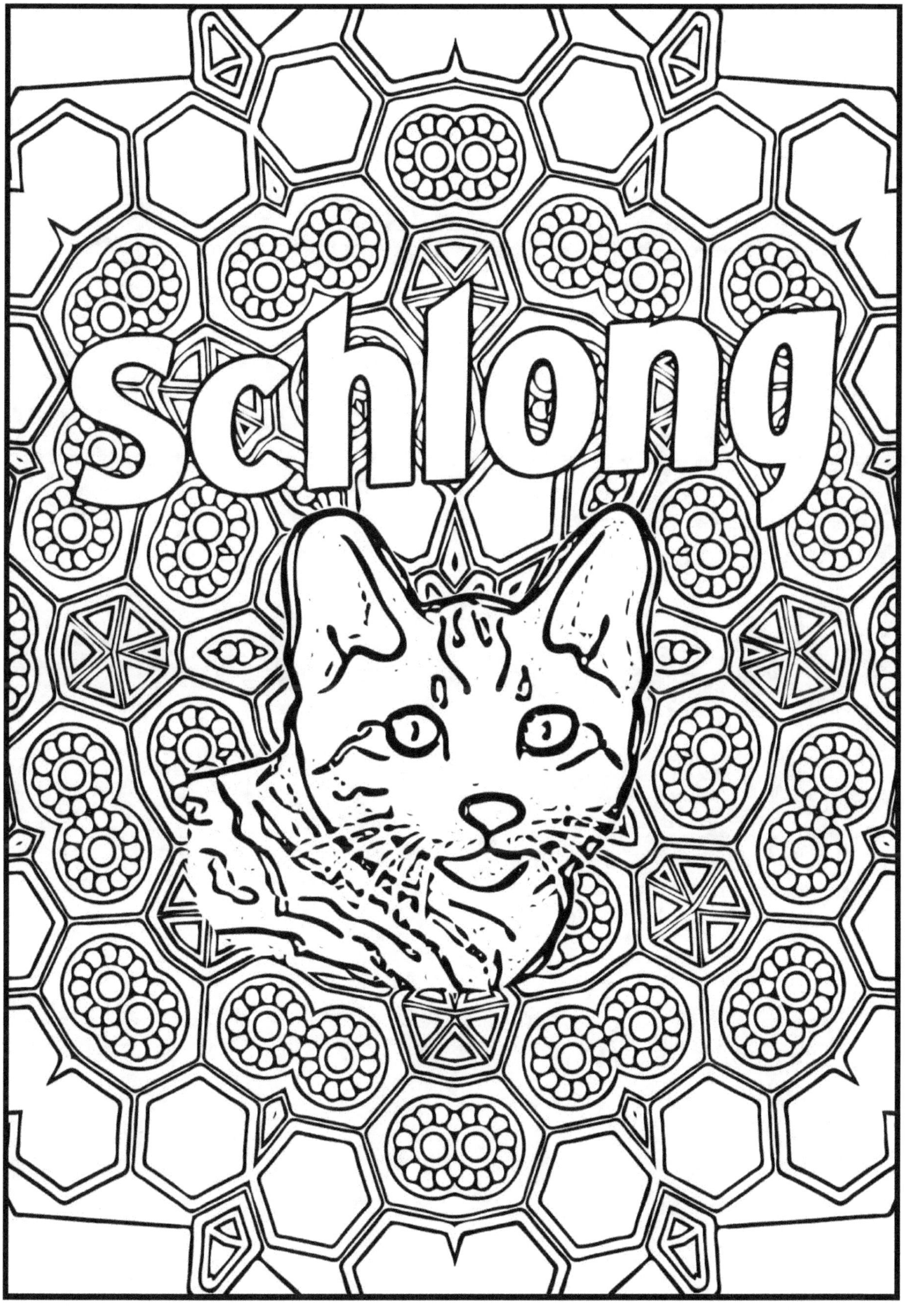
Schlong

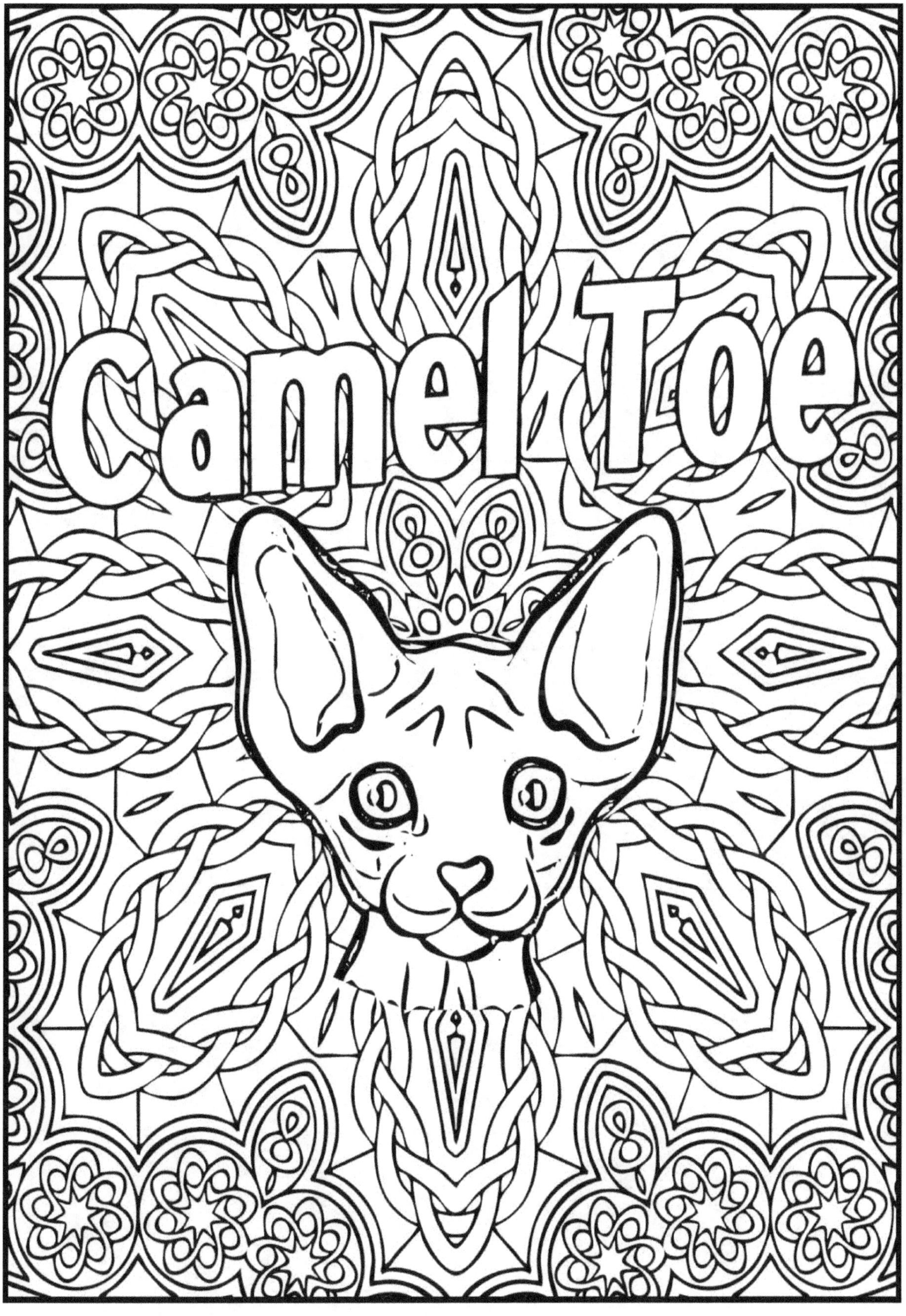
Camel Toe

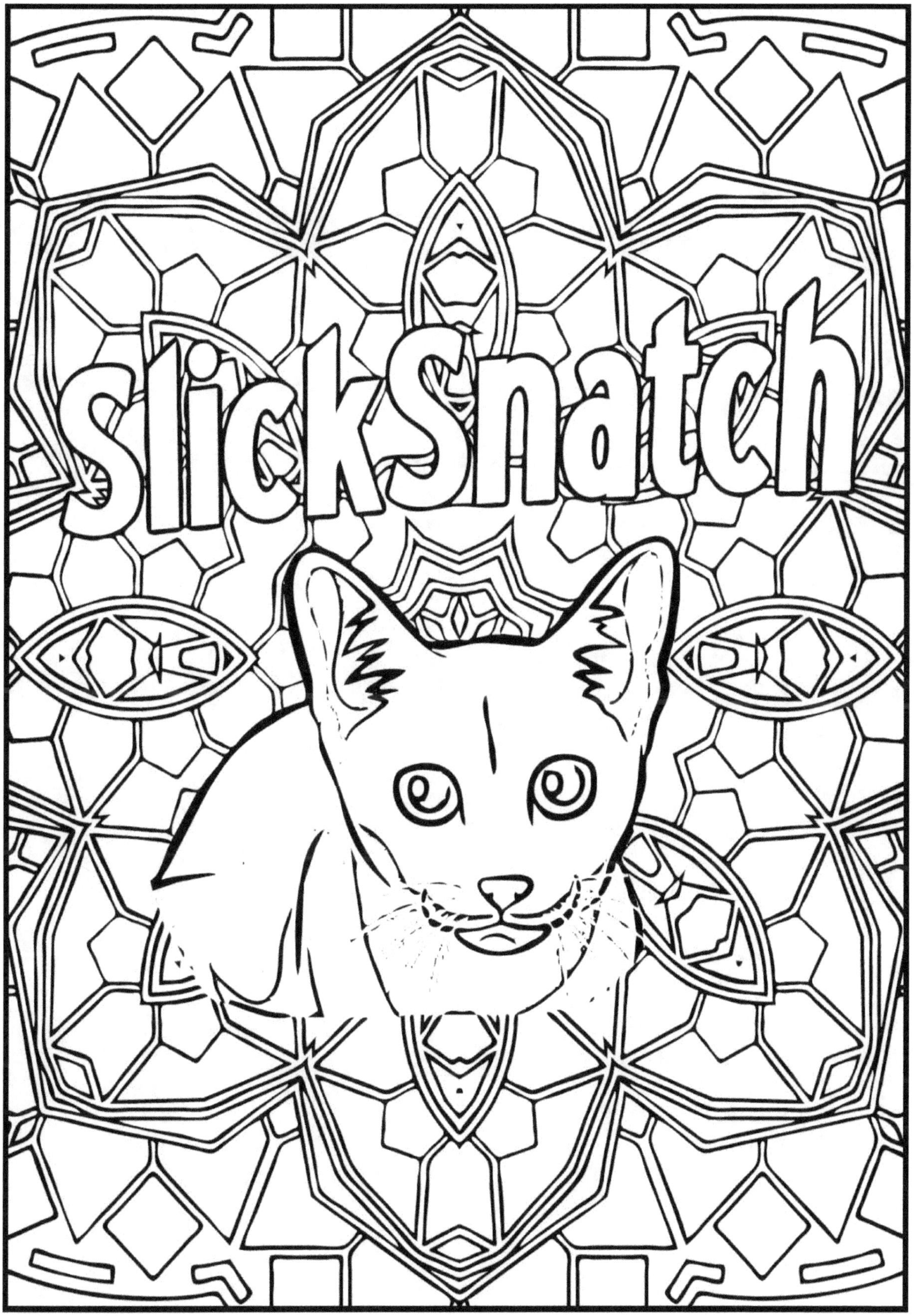
Slick Snatch

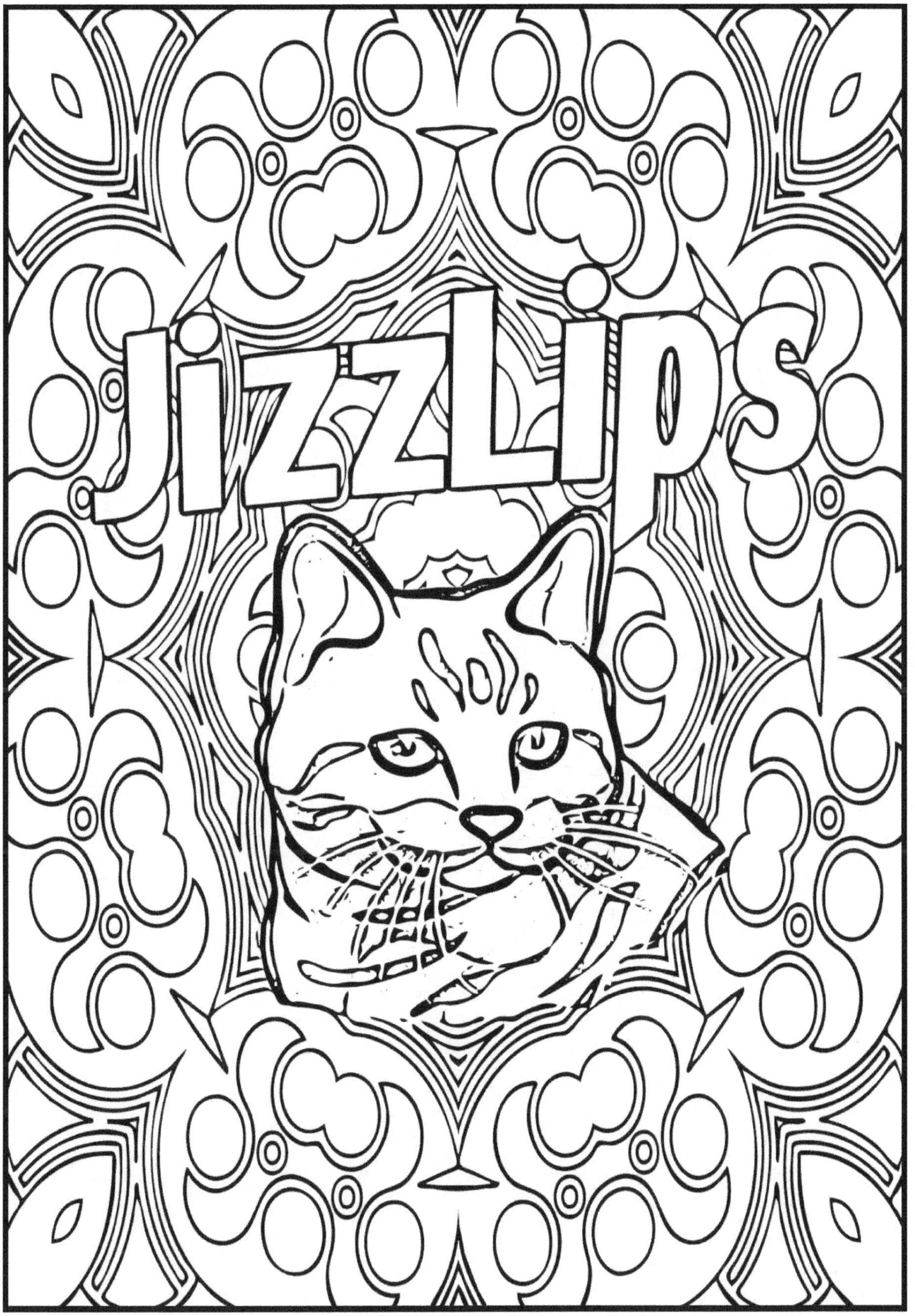
JiZZLips

www.ingramcontent.com/pod-product-compliance
Lightning Source LLC
Chambersburg PA
CBHW080612190526
45169CB00007B/2977